my very first

famous paintings

Rosie Dickins

Designed by
Josephine Thompson
and Nicola Butler

With cartoons by
Carles Ballesteros

Details from Yoko and the Tiger, pages 18–19

About this book

This book is full of famous paintings from different times and places. You can find out about the pictures, spot hidden details and try out some of the techniques used by the artists.

Usborne Quicklinks

For links to websites where you can explore lots more famous paintings, and learn more about the paintings in this book, go to www.usborne.com/quicklinks and type in the title of this book.

Children – ask an adult's permission before using the internet.

What you will need

Here is a list of the things you will need to try out the techniques in this book.

Pens and pencils
Chalks and crayons
Paints and brushes
Plain and coloured paper
Old magazines and wrapping paper
Polystyrene or foam packaging
Sweets and wrappers
Plastic fork
Scissors and glue

Contents

Eye-catching colours

In this picture, a long, purple road winds
steeply downhill and into the distance –
drawing your eye into the picture with it.

Garrowby Hill by David Hockney

The fields surrounding the road form a colourful patchwork.
Notice how some of the patches seem brighter and more
zingy than others, and how they pull your eye towards them.

4

Some pairs of colours look extra bright when you see them side-by-side. Artists call these 'complementary' colours. Here are some of them.

red and green

purple and yellow

blue and orange

You can see how complementary colours were used in the painting on the right. The colours almost seem to glow – making everything look hot and sunny.

The Turning Road, L'Estaque by Andre Derain

Try it yourself

Draw some stripy hills with wax crayons.

Then paint over them in contrasting colours.

Portrait of a lady

Over 500 years ago, a famous Italian artist
was hired to paint a famous Italian beauty.

Lady with an Ermine by Leonardo da Vinci

Can you spot?

A see-through veil,
edged with gold
thread, covering
her forehead.

Her plain black
beads which – like
her simple dress –
show she was not
from a particularly
rich family.

Gold letters
spelling out the
title (in French)
and the artist's
name, in the top
left corner.

The picture shows 16-year-old Cecilia Gallerani, a favourite at the court of a powerful Italian duke. She is holding an animal known as an ermine. With its pure white fur, the ermine was meant to show how pure and good she was.

Artist Leonardo da Vinci didn't have a real ermine to look at, so he made one up based on other drawings.

The ermine's paws were probably based on a dog's paws, like these.

Dog
by Leonardo da Vinci

To make his paintings as lifelike as possible, Leonardo filled sketchbook after sketchbook with nature drawings and notes – as well as some amazing inventions.

Sleeping cat

Flying machine

Dragon

Masks

Untitled (Mask: Wild Animal) by Paul Klee

With its wonky eyes and toothy grin, this looks like
the face of a monster or wild animal. But according
to the artist, it is just a mask – so there could be
someone much less fierce hiding behind it.

Artist Paul Klee may have been inspired by African masks like this one. Masks were meant to look as impressive as possible. So all the features are bold and exaggerated – just like Klee's picture.

This mask was carved out of wood, then decorated with feathers, straw and paint.

African masks were supposed to hold magical powers, and were worn only on special occasions.

Ceremonial Mask by an unknown artist from the Ivory Coast, West Africa

Try it yourself

Try designing your own mask, using shapes cut from old wrapping paper or magazines.

Arrange the shapes to make a face, then glue them down.

9

Magical tales

This bright, happy picture was inspired by a book of magical tales from the Middle East, known as *The Thousand and One Nights*.

The Thousand and One Nights by Henri Matisse

The tales include "Aladdin and the Magic Lamp". Can you see two magic lamps... and wisps of smoke that might be genies?

The story went that a young queen invented the tales to entertain a sleepless king. She would talk through the night and stop at dawn. So the artist included the words (in French): "She saw the light of day and fell silent."

The picture is decorated with hearts, to show the king and queen's love for each other.

The artist, Henri Matisse, was too ill to stand up and paint. So he cut shapes out of coloured paper instead. He called this 'drawing with scissors'.

Try it yourself

Use scissors to snip different shapes out of paper, and glue them down to make a picture.

You could cut spiky shapes, like stars...

...or wiggly shapes, like leaves.

Children's Games by Pieter Bruegel

Playing games

This 450-year-old painting shows a town square packed with children playing. The artist wanted to show as many of their games as possible.

Can you spot?

There are about 80 separate games in the picture — many still popular today. How many can you recognize?

climbing

blind man's buff

making music

tag

marbles

bowls

jacks

tug of war

Abstract art

On White II by Wassily Kandinsky

This picture is like a colourful explosion.
Bold black lines and bright, spiky shapes contrast
dramatically with the plain white background.

The artist, Wassily Kandinsky, often compared painting to music.

He believed looking at
shapes and colours could
make you feel emotions,
in the same way as
listening to music.

Pictures like this, which don't try to show real people,
things or scenes, are often described as 'abstract' art.

Try it yourself

Try making your own abstract art
by arranging things you can find.
We've used sweets and wrappers.

Chair portrait

The artist's pipe and tobacco lie on the seat.

Notice the sunny yellow patches on the chair. Yellow was the artist's favourite colour.

Van Gogh's Chair by Vincent van Gogh

This might look like a picture of a chair. But it's also a kind of self portrait. The artist, Vincent van Gogh, chose a plain kitchen chair. It suggests someone plain and down to earth – which is just how van Gogh saw himself.

Compare the first chair with this one – which van Gogh painted for his friend, Paul Gauguin. It's an elegant chair with books on it, suggesting an elegant, thoughtful person.

A lit candle adds a dreamy, night-time feeling.

Gauguin's Chair
by Vincent van Gogh

Both pictures are painted in thick, bumpy layers of paint. The paint is so thick, you can see the marks left by van Gogh's brush.

Try it yourself

Mix some ready-mix paint with pva glue, to thicken it.

Use a big brush to paint thick swirls and stripes.

You can scrape lines in the paint with a plastic fork.

Tiger print

This striking scene was printed over 150 years ago in Japan.

The print shows a brave boy named Yoko, chasing a tiger away from his father. It was part of a series of pictures about children helping their parents.

Yoko and the Tiger by Utagawa Kuniyoshi

Kuniyoshi was one of Japan's most famous print artists. He used carved wooden blocks to make his prints.

Printing meant he could make and sell lots of copies of each picture.

The story is told in the panel full of Japanese writing.

揚香

Try it yourself

Draw a shape on a piece of polystyrene or foam packaging.

'Carve' the lines by pushing a ballpoint pen into the foam.

Brush paint over your carving, then press it onto paper.

Curved lines sweep across the picture, showing gusts of wind.

The carved lines stay white.

Painting movement

At first sight, this painting is a jumble of shapes and colours. But if you look carefully, you can make out a woman in a blue dress.

The woman's arms appear several times.

The artist glued real sequins onto her dress.

Blue Dancer by Gino Severini

Paintings can't move – so how can an artist make something *look* as if it's moving? The woman in blue is a whirling, twirling dancer. The artist painted her as a lot of broken shapes, to try to capture her movement.

The picture on the left shows a woman walking her dog. This artist used a blur of repeated shapes to show the movement of their feet.

Dynamism of a Dog on a Leash
by Giacomo Balla

Cartoon artists often use a similar trick. They add 'movement lines' to show something moving.

Try it yourself

Try adding repeated shapes and movement lines to your own drawings.

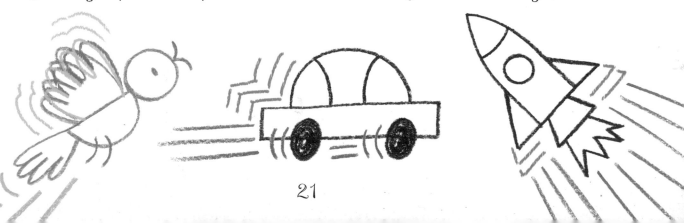

21

Big flowers

Oriental Poppies by Georgia O'Keeffe

The poppies in this rich, red picture have been painted about ten times bigger than life. They fill the frame - so there is nothing to distract from the flowers themselves.

The zoomed-in view really makes you look carefully at the poppies. Up close, you can see every detail. Notice how the silky red petals change from scarlet to pink and orange.

The changing colours were built up out of thin, smooth layers of paint.

Artist (and New York resident) Georgia O'Keeffe said: "Nobody takes time to see a flower, really, it is so small... So I said to myself... I'll paint it big... I'll make even busy New Yorkers take time to see what I see of flowers."

Try it yourself

You can try colour mixing with thin layers of tissue paper.

Tear out shapes and glue them down in overlapping layers.

When the glue is dry, you can draw on top in pen.

Little angels

This picture of two baby angels, or cherubs, is often seen on its own. But it is really part of a bigger picture, which includes Mary, the baby Jesus and two saints. You can see the whole picture underneath.

Detail of The Sistine Madonna by Raphael

The cherubs look slightly bored – just like real children. The story goes that the artist based them on two little boys who were waiting in his studio while he painted their mother.

The Sistine Madonna by Raphael

Notice how the picture is framed by heavy green curtains. They make it feel as if we're peeking through a window, rather than looking at a painting.

Can you spot?

- A wedding-cake-shaped hat in one corner; it belonged to the saint on the left and shows he used to be a pope.

- The faces of more cherubs, just visible in the clouds in the background.

Doodle birds

This picture is like a bright, cheerful doodle. Can you see some bird-like creatures among the shapes and lines?

Bird People by Joan Miro

The bright colours and lively bird-creatures make the picture look bright and cheerful. Artist Joan Miro often meant his art as a celebration of life. After Miro had finished the design, it was turned into a huge outdoor mosaic, using a million pieces of glass and marble.

The picture probably started out as a doodle. Miro believed that doodling – or drawing without thinking about it – was a way of letting deeper, more basic parts of his mind shape his art.

Try it yourself

Doodle some loopy shapes.

Add eyes and noses or beaks.

Don't worry about being too neat.

Colour them in bright colours.

At the circus

This lively circus scene was painted in Paris over a hundred years ago.

The Circus by Georges Seurat

The artist, Georges Seurat, was inspired by circus posters like this one – which he would have seen all over Paris.

If you look closely, you'll see Seurat's painting is made of coloured dots. He thought the contrasts between the colours would make them seem brighter.

Each dot was dabbed on with the tip of a brush.

Use a mix of colours.

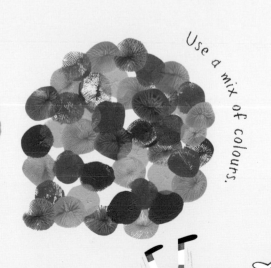

Try it yourself

Draw a shape in pencil. Then dip a finger in paint and fill the shape with dots.

Painting sunshine

This boating scene was painted outside, to capture the effect of the sunshine on a bright summer's day.

Red Boat, Argenteuil by Pierre-Auguste Renoir

Notice the little dog watching from the jetty.

The artist used dashes of orange, yellow, pink and green to give the blue water extra sparkle.

The picture on the right also uses bright colours to show sunlight gleaming on water. How many colours can you spot in the ripples?

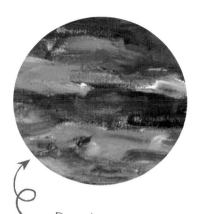

Rough, wavy brushmarks add to the rippling effect.

Summertime by Mary Cassatt

Try it yourself

Draw long, wavy lines in blue and green. Leave some paper showing.

Add short dashes of other colours, such as orange, yellow and pink.

You could draw some fish between the waves, too.

Splattery art

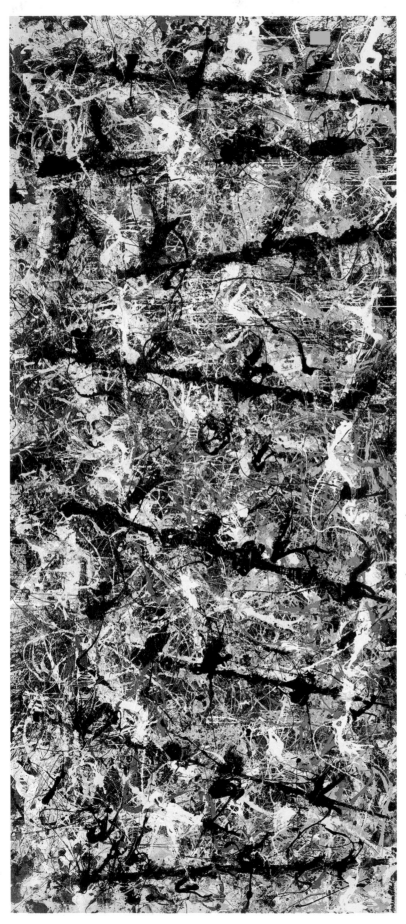

Blue Poles by Jackson Pollock

The picture was first known simply as Number 11. It was later named Blue Poles after the blue lines which dance across it.

This picture is like a tangled web of paint, filled with streaks and splashes of bright colour.

Artist Jackson Pollock made the picture by splashing, squirting, dripping and pouring different colours of paint onto a base laid flat on the floor.

Pollock was nicknamed Jack the Dripper, because of his unusual way of painting.

The blue lines were added near the end, probably with a piece of wood dipped in paint. The result might look messy, but it is full of energy and rhythm.

Looking closely, people have spotted footprints

and even bits of broken glass in the paint.

Keep dipping and flicking, in different colours.

Try it yourself

Dip a brush in runny paint and flick it over your paper.

Spread out old newspapers or do the flicking outside.

A Dream of the Past: Sir Isumbras at the Ford by John Everett Millais

Knight in armour

This painting shows an old knight in golden armour, carrying two poor children across a river – showing that a good knight should help the weak.

The background is beautifully painted to suggest a golden evening light. The women in black and white are meant to be nuns – a reminder of religion and its importance to the knight.

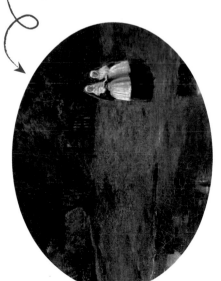

If you look closely at the horse, its body is oddly long. Some writers compared it to a donkey!

The artist probably made it bigger on purpose, to make more room for the children.

Can you spot?

- Some peacock feathers by the knight's sword.

- The children's bare feet – they are too poor to have any shoes.

- A bundle of sticks on the boy's back – the children have been gathering firewood.

Matchstick people

This 60-year-old painting shows a grimy city, full of smoking chimneys. Strolling people bring the scene to life.

The Pond by L.S. Lowry

Artist L.S. Lowry taught himself to paint. He became known for his simple way of drawing people. Art writers called them 'matchstick men'.

Can you spot two black dogs in the painting?

36

Lowry made up the view. But he filled it with real-life details, including a long, arched railway bridge on the right.

Look out for the train puffing across the top.

The bridge was near Lowry's home in the north of England.

The people seem to be relaxing, bobbing about in boats or strolling over the hills. But the tall factory chimneys are there to remind us work is never very far away.

Try it yourself

To draw a matchstick man, start with a round head. Add a body. Then draw lines for the arms and legs.

You could make your people do different things, such as waving, walking or ice-skating.

Animals

This picture, by famous animal artist
Edwin Landseer, contrasts two very different dogs:
a big, sad-eyed bloodhound and a cheeky little terrier.

The big dog was
called Grafton,
and the little one
was called Scratch.
This picture
was painted for
their owner.

Landseer became so
famous for painting
dogs that he had a
breed named after him.

Dignity and Impudence by Edwin Landseer

smooth

fluffy

Notice how the fur is painted. The big dog's soft, smooth fur is painted with soft, smooth brushstrokes. The fluffy little dog is all rough dabs and lines.

This is another famous animal picture. It shows a hare, painted in amazing detail. Lots of tiny lines give the look of thick, ruffled fur.

You can just make out a window reflected in the hare's eye.

Hare by Albrecht Durer

Try it yourself

Draw a simple animal outline.

Fill it with smooth shading, for smooth fur...

...or scribbly lines, for fluffy fur.

Windy weather

Woman with a Parasol by Claude Monet

Artist Claude Monet painted this picture outdoors, to capture the effect of the weather. Swirling brushstrokes give everything a windswept look.

Try it yourself

Try drawing swirling
lines for wind...

...rows
of curls for
crashing waves...

...or slanting
lines for rain.

Monet was a big fan of the artist J.M.W. Turner,
who painted this dramatic storm at sea...

Rockets and Blue Lights (Close at Hand) to Warn
Steamboats of Shoal Water by J.M.W. Turner

Huge waves crash on the shore, and the sky is lit up by blue
emergency flares. Rough, choppy brushstrokes make the picture
feel even more stormy.

Clowns

This picture, by Pablo Picasso, shows his son Paul dressed up as a type of French clown called Pierrot.

Portrait of Paul as Pierrot by Pablo Picasso

The Pierrot picture is delicately painted. Smudgey colours give it a soft, pretty look. But Picasso didn't always paint like this...

Here is another of Picasso's clowns, painted very differently. Blocky, overlapping shapes create a deliberately flat, geometric effect.

Harlequin
by Pablo Picasso

Notice the bright diamonds. This clown, called Harlequin, always wore a diamond-patterned suit.

Pierrot always wore white. He was a gentle clown, who often got his heart broken.

Try it yourself

You can try smudgy colours yourself, using chalk.
Draw a round shape and rub it gently with a finger.

You could add a face on top in pen.

Home life

Painted over 350 years ago, this picture shows
a maid pouring milk from a jug – an ordinary scene,
captured in extraordinary detail.

The Milkmaid by Jan Vermeer

The maid is probably mixing bread and milk to make a pudding.

The artist painted everything just as it looked – even old nails and dirt on the walls. The food on the table could almost be a photograph.

Each speck of light is shown as a tiny dot of white paint.

When this was painted, you couldn't buy paints in shops. So artists had to make their own colours. The rich blue of the maid's apron was made from crushed blue gemstones.

Try it yourself

Crush a small piece of coloured chalk with a spoon.

Mix in a little bit of water and a drop of glue.

Try painting with the mixture.

Cartoon battle

This bold, colourful painting of a mid-air battle
was based on a 1960s American comic.

Whaam! by Roy Lichtenstein

The picture was painted on two panels, a bit like
the boxes in a cartoon strip. The trace of
a rocket blast links the two panels together.

Each panel was designed in old-fashioned comic-book style, using bold black lines and only a few colours.

Can you spot?

If you look closely, you can see how some of the colours are made up of tiny dots – like the dots used to print comics.

But unlike a comic, these dots were carefully painted by hand.

ACKNOWLEDGEMENTS

Additional illustrations by Josephine Thompson, Antonia Miller, Nicola Butler and Katie Lovell. Step artwork by Vicky Arrowsmith. Additional photographic manipulation by John Russell. Edited by Jane Chisholm and Jenny Tyler. Art Director: Mary Cartwright.

Cover: Detail from Untitled (Mask: Wild Animal), see credit for pages 8-9. Detail from Circus, see credit for pages 28-29. Red Boat, Argenteuil see credit for pages 30-31. Portrait of Paul as Pierrot see credit for pages 42-43. Title page: Details from Yoko and the Tiger, see credit for pages 18-19. Pages 4-5: Garrowby Hill (1998) by Hockney, oil on canvas, 60 x 76in © David Hockney, collection Museum of Fine Arts, Boston; photo credit: Prudence Cuming Associates. Turning Road, L'Estaque (1906) by Derain, oil on canvas © ADAGP, Paris and DACS, London 2012; digital image © Museum of Fine Arts, Houston, Texas, USA/ Gift of Audrey Jones Beck/ Bridgeman Art Library. Pages 6-7: Lady with an Ermine (Cecilia Gallerani) (1496) by Leonardo, oil on walnut panel © Czartoryski Museum, Cracow, Poland/ Bridgeman Art Library. Dog (c.1480) by Leonardo, detail from Study of a dog and a cat, metalpoint on paper, British Museum, London, UK/ Bridgeman Art Library. Sleeping cat and Dragon (c.1513-16) by Leonardo, details from Cats, lions and a dragon, pen & ink with wash over blue chalk, Royal Collection © 2011 Her Majesty Queen Elizabeth II/ Bridgeman Art Library. Flying machine (1488-90) by Leonardo, detail from Flying Machines, fol. 83v from Paris Manuscript B, pen and ink on paper, Bibliotheque de l'Institut de France, Paris, France/ Alinari/ Bridgeman Art Library. Pages 8-9: Untitled (Mask: Wild Animal) (c.1939) by Klee, coloured pencil & coloured paste on paper, Zentrum Paul Klee, Bern, Switzerland/ Bridgeman Art Library. Ceremonial mask (late 19th century) by unknown Wobe or Grebo artist, Ivory Coast, wood, feathers & fibres, Musee de l'Homme, Paris, France/ Bridgeman Art Library. Pages 10-11: The Thousand and One Nights (1950) by Matisse, gouache on paper, cut and pasted, 53.75 x 147.25in, Carnegie Museum of Art, Pittsburgh, acquired through the generosity of the Sarah Mellon Scaife Family © Succession H. Matisse/ DACS 2012; photograph © 2012 Carnegie Museum of Art, Pittsburgh. Photo of Henri Matisse at Home (c.1949) by Clifford Coffin © Condé Nast Archive/ Corbis. Pages 12-13: Children's Games (Kinderspiele) (1560) by Bruegel, oil on panel, Kunsthistorisches Museum, Vienna, Austria/ Bridgeman Art Library. Pages 14-15: On White II or Auf Weiss II (1923) (Roethel 694) by Kandinsky, oil on canvas © ADAGP, Paris and DACS, London 2012; digital image © White Images/ Scala, Florence. Pages 16-17: Van Gogh's Chair (1888) by van Gogh, oil on canvas, National Gallery, London, England; photo © Corbis. Gauguin's Chair (1888) by van Gogh, oil on canvas, Van Gogh Museum, Amsterdam, Netherlands; photo © Corbis. Pages 18-19: Yoko and the Tiger from 'Twenty-four Paragons of Filial Piety' ('Nijushi Ko doji Kagami'), pub. c.1840 by Kuniyoshi, colour woodblock print, Private Collection/ Bridgeman Art Library. Pages 20-21: Blue Dancer (1912) by Severini, oil on canvas with sequins © ADAGP, Paris and DACS, London 2012; digital image © Mattioli Collection, Milan, Italy/ Giraudon/ Bridgeman Art Library. Dynamism of a Dog on a Leash (1912) by Balla, oil on canvas © DACS 2012; digital image © Albright Knox Art Gallery, Buffalo, New York, USA/ Bridgeman Art Library. Pages 22-23: Oriental Poppies (1927) by O'Keeffe, oil on canvas, 30 x 40 1/8 in, Frederick R. Weisman Art Museum © Georgia O'Keeffe Museum/ DACS, London 2012; photo © Collection of Frederick R. Weisman Art Museum at University of Minnesota, Minneapolis, Museum Purchase 1937.1. Pages 24-25: Sistine Madonna (1513) by Raphael, oil on canvas, Gemaeldegalerie Alte Meister, Dresden, Germany © Staatliche Kunstsammlungen Dresden/ Bridgeman Art Library. Pages 26-27: Bird People (1974-76) by Miro © Succession Miro/ ADAGP, Paris and DACS, London 2012; photo © Christie's Images/ CORBIS. Pages 28-29: Circus (1891) by Seurat, oil on canvas © White Images/ Scala, Florence. Poster advertising 'Fernando Circus', Paris (19th century) by an unknown French artist, colour litho, Bibliotheque Historique de la Ville de Paris, Paris, France/ Archives Charmet/ Bridgeman Art Library. Pages 30-31: Red Boat, Argenteuil (1888) by Renoir, oil on canvas, Barnes Foundation, Merion, Pennsylvania, USA/ Bridgeman Art Library. Summertime (c.1894) by Cassatt, oil on canvas © Terra Foundation for American Art, Chicago/ Art Resource, NY. Pages 32-33: Blue Poles (1952) by Pollock, oil, enamel, aluminium paint & glass on canvas © The Pollock-Krasner Foundation ARS, NY and DACS, London 2012; digital image © National Gallery of Australia, Canberra (purchased 1973)/ Bridgeman Art Library. Pages 34-35: A Dream of the Past: Sir Isumbras at the Ford (1857) by Millais, oil on canvas © Lady Lever Art Gallery, National Museums Liverpool/ Bridgeman Art Library. Pages 36-37: Pond (1950) by Lowry, oil on canvas © The Estate of L.S. Lowry, All Rights Reserved, DACS 2012; digital image © Tate, London 2012. Pages 38-39: Dignity and Impudence (1839) by Landseer, oil on canvas, digital image © Tate, London 2012. Hare (1502) by Durer, watercolour on paper, Graphische Sammlung Albertina, Vienna, Austria/ Bridgeman Art Library. Pages 40-41: Woman with a Parasol - Madam Monet and Her Son (1875) by Monet, oil on canvas, National Gallery of Art, Washington DC, USA/ Photo © AISA/ Bridgeman Art Library. Rockets and Blue Lights (Close at Hand) to Warn Steamboats of Shoal Water (1840) by Turner, oil on canvas, Sterling & Francine Clark Art Institute, Williamstown, USA/ Bridgeman Art Library. Pages 42-43: Portrait of Paul as Pierrot or Paul en Pierrot a Fleurs (12/07/1929) by Picasso, oil on canvas © Succession Picasso/ DACS, London 2012; digital image © Private Collection/ Peter Willi/ Bridgeman Art Library. Harlequin (1915) by Picasso, oil on canvas © Succession Picasso/DACS, London 2012; digital image © Museum of Modern Art, New York, USA / Bridgeman Art Library. Pages 44-45: Milkmaid (c.1658-60) by Vermeer, oil on canvas, Rijksmuseum, Amsterdam, Netherlands/ Bridgeman Art Library. Pages 46-47: Whaam! (1963) by Lichtenstein, acrylic & oil on canvas © The Estate of Roy Lichtenstein/ DACS 2012; digital image © Tate, London 2012.

First published in 2013 by Usborne Publishing Ltd., Usborne House, 83-85 Saffron Hill, London ECIN 8RT, England. www.usborne.com Copyright © 2013 Usborne Publishing Ltd. UKE